The
Wright
Brothers

The Birth of
Modern Aviation

Anna Sproule

BLACKBIRCH PRESS, INC.
WOODBRIDGE, CONNECTICUT

Published by Blackbirch Press, Inc.
260 Amity Road
Woodbridge, CT 06525
web site: http://www.blackbirch.com
e-mail: staff@blackbirch.com

© 1999 Blackbirch Press, Inc.
First U.S. Edition

First published in Great Britain by Exley Publications Ltd., Chalk Hill, Watford, 1990.
© Exley Publications Ltd.
© Anna Sproule

10 9 8 7 6 5 4 3 2 1   Printed in China

Photo Credits

Cover: Wright State University Library.
Austin Brown/Aviation Picture Library: 23, 47, 58
(below); The Bettmann Archive: 6–7, 33, 35, 44;
The Bridgeman Art Library: 54–55; Mary Evans
Picture Library: 4, 9, 12, 24, 50–51, 56–57; Exley
Publications Photo Library: 16–17 (Nick Birch);
Henry Ford Museum: 26, 39, 53; Library of
Congress: 28, 34, 37, 40; NHPA: 30–31 (Manfred
Daneggar), 43 (Stephen Dalton); Popperfoto: 31;
Ann Ronan Picture Library: 11, 18–21; The Royal
Aeronautical Society: 49; The Science Museum:
10; The Science Photo Library: 38 (Dale Boyer/
NASA), 39 (Dr. Gary Settles), 58 (John Ross);
The Smithsonian Institution: 48, Townley Hall Art
Gallery and Museum: 13; Zeta: 59.

Acknowledgements

Extracts from *The Conquest of the Air* by C.L.M.
Brown, OUP, 1927, reprinted with permission of
Oxford University Press.

Extracts from *Interpretive History of Flight* by
M.J.B. Davy, reprinted with permission of the
Science Museum.

Extracts from *The Papers of Wilbur and Orville
Wright,* ed. Marvin W. McFarland, McGraw-Hill,
1953.

Extracts from *The Wright Brothers: Heirs of
Prometheus,* ed. R. Hallion, published by the
National Aeronautical & Space Center (originally
published in *Flying and the Aero Club of America
Bulletin,* 1913).

Extracts from *Airborne at Kitty Hawk* by Michael
Harrington, reprinted with permission of
MacMillan Publishing Company (originally
published by Cassell & Co. Ltd, London, 1953).

Extracts from *The Wright Brothers* by Fred C.
Kelly, reprinted with permisison of Harrap
Publishing Group Ltd and Harcourt, Brace
Jovanovich Inc.

Library of Congress Cataloging-in-Publication Data

Sproule, Anna.
    The Wright brothers: The birth of modern aviation / by Anna Sproule.
        p. cm.—(Giants of Science)
    Includes bibliographical references and index.
    Summary: A biography of the brothers who made the world's first flight in a
power-driven, heavier-than-air machine at Kitty Hawk, North Carolina, in 1903.
    ISBN 1-56711-328-1
    1. Wright, Orville, 1871–1948—Juvenile literature. 2. Wright, Wilbur, 1867–1912—
Juvenile literature. 3. Aeronautics—United States—Biography—Juvenile literature. [1. Wright,
Orville, 1871–1948. 2. Wright, Wilbur, 1867–1912. 3. Aeronautics—Biography.] I. Title.
II. Series.
TL540.W7S63   1999   98–49139
629.13'0092'2—dc21   CIP
[b]   AC

Contents

Le Petit Journal

Le Petit Journal
CHAQUE JOUR — 6 PAGES — 5 CENTIMES
Administration : 61, rue Lafayette
Les manuscrits ne sont pas rendus

5 CENTIMES **SUPPLÉMENT ILLUSTRÉ** **5** CENTIMES

Le Petit Journal agricole, 5 cent. ~~ La Mode du Petit Journal, 10 cent.
Le Petit Journal illustré de la Jeunesse, 10 cent.
On s'abonne sans frais dans tous les bureaux de poste

ABONNEMENTS

	SIX MOIS	UN AN
SEINE et SEINE-ET-OISE..	2 fr.	3 fr. 50
DÉPARTEMENTS..........	2 fr.	4 fr. »
ÉTRANGER..............	2 50	5 fr. »

Dix-neuvième Année

DIMANCHE 30 AOUT 1908

Numéro 928

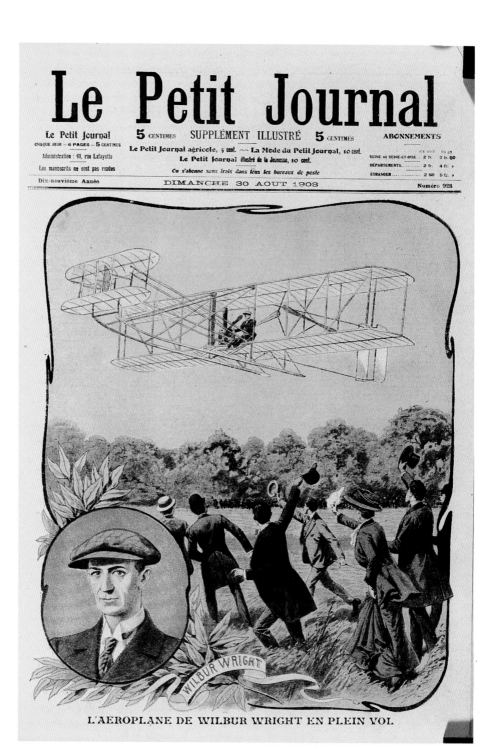

L'AEROPLANE DE WILBUR WRIGHT EN PLEIN VOL

Flight of Fancy

From the doorway of their hut, the two brothers watched as the wind came roaring out of the north across the sand flats, driving sheets of loose sand before it.

In its shed close by, their flying machine waited, trembling in the wind that gusted through the timbers. It had already survived one crash on a gentle day. But today—December 17—the wind was roaring over the North Carolina coast at a speed approaching gale force.

Watching the twirling sand-devils, one of the men suddenly spoke. "We won't have to climb the hill. We can launch it from here."

The other one nodded. It was true. To get up enough speed for the first launch, they had started the machine on a sand dune. It had run downhill, taken off—and stalled. Today, though, the wind would do the work. It would fling the machine up like a kite, thrust it forward by an engine, ready to challenge gravity and fly where it wished.

The two men had designed the engine themselves. They had designed every part of the aircraft that waited for them in the shed—experimenting, researching, testing their findings. Now, just one great experiment remained.

Opposite: *The aircraft shown on the cover was demonstrated in France in 1908. Its pilot was an American named Wilbur Wright who, with his brother, had built the first successful full-sized airplane only five years earlier.*

5

Wilbur Wright

"Go On, Orville"

On that gusty day, the Wrights bustled their little camp into life. They checked the wind again. They hung up a symbol to call the lifeguards from their base a mile away across the sand. The lifeguards had been in on the plan from the start; they couldn't be left out now.

Next came the machine itself. Its builders hauled it out of the shed and checked it over. The wings, the struts, the wires that linked the controls: they were all as they should be. The propellers moved easily. So did the lever that controlled the front rudder, sticking out in front of the wings. The sled-like runners on which the machine stood showed no sign of the accident a few days earlier.

The Wrights arranged it on its launching rail, and anchored it with a length of wire. To keep it steady, Wilbur shoved a prop under its right-hand wing. A few feet away, Orville set up his camera. As he settled the tripod's legs firmly into the stand, the lifeguards hurried into the camp, excited by what they were about to witness.

They watched intently as the two brothers started the engine. It ran with a steady, reassuring throb, warming up for the moment when it would take the machine down the rail and into the air.

"Go on, Orville," Wilbur said. "I've had my turn. It's yours now." Cautiously, Orville eased himself into the machine, and stretched out flat on the lower wing. The wind gusted straight into his eyes.

In a last check of the controls, he moved his hips gently from side to side. The cradle in which he lay shifted with him, twisting and dipping the wing surfaces at his sides. At the end of the right-hand wing stood Wilbur, waiting to steady it as the machine moved down the rail.

It was really time to go now. Orville reached out and released the machine's wire anchor.

In Free Flight

Orville was moving forward at walking pace. From the corner of his eye, he could see his brother jogging alongside the aircraft. Beginning to run. . . . And, suddenly, Wilbur wasn't there anymore.

The machine was airborne!

But it was going too high. Quickly, Orville moved the lever that led to the front rudder. Instantly, he was heading toward the ground, only ten feet below him. Desperately, he dragged the lever back.

With a sickening jolt, the aircraft halted its crazy plunge. The earth fell away, as the machine surged upward again. A gust caught its wings and sent him soaring even higher.

Orville touched the lever. With dizzying speed, the machine tilted in the air. Then it swooped for the ground. Another correction, and it tilted up again. And down. And up. . . .

And down. With a crunch, a final crashing jolt, and a great spray of sand, the machine slammed into a swirling dune. Dazed and breathless, Orville crawled out of the aircraft and looked back along the way he had come.

Orville Wright

Humans in Air

He had only flown 120 feet (36.5 meters). He had only been airborne for 12 seconds. But that short distance and tiny timespan added up to nothing less than an extraordinary human victory.

Orville and his brother had gone where no one had ever gone before. They had built a heavier-than-air machine that could carry a person in free flight. It kept itself in the air by its own power, and its movement could be controlled—roughly, but still decisively—by its pilot. Between them, they had designed and created the world's first successful full-sized airplane.

"To Wilbur and Orville Wright—whose courage made it possible—was left the final glory of producing the first successful flying machine. They succeeded, by their own exertions, in doing what others were mainly thinking and talking about."

—M.J.B. Davy, from "Interpretive History of Flight"

On the sands of South Kitty Hawk, North Carolina, Wilbur and Orville Wright had conquered the air.

"First in the History of the World"

Looking back at that December day nearly 100 years ago, it is easy to see why the Wrights' achievement was so momentous.

Orville's own report, published in 1913, still remains the best way of defining what the brothers had achieved. "This flight," he wrote, "only lasted twelve seconds, but it was nevertheless the first in the history of the world in which a machine carrying a man had raised itself by its own power into the air in full flight, had sailed forward without reduction of speed, and had finally landed at a point as high as that from which it started."

Every word in Orville's statement is important—and what Orville doesn't say is as important as what he does. For instance, he doesn't say he was the first man to fly. That record had been taken over 100 years earlier by two Frenchmen, Pilatre de Rozier and the Marquis of Arlandes.

Nor does Orville claim to have designed the first machine to leave the ground successfully. It was another pair of brothers who had done that. Also French, they were two paper manufacturers named Joseph and Étienne Montgolfier. In the early 1780s, the Montgolfiers had started experimenting with the properties of hot air. In June 1783, they filled a large balloon of cloth and paper with hot air and released it. The balloon soared skyward, and rose to the tremendous height of 6,000 feet (1,829 meters). When the air inside it cooled, it returned to earth over a mile away. There, it was quickly ripped up by terrified peasants, who thought it was sent by the Devil.

Top left: *In a test of the effect of flight on living creatures, a hot-air balloon designed by the Montgolfier brothers of France made a trial flight over Versailles in the 1780s. The basket contained a sheep, a rooster, and a duck. The sheep stepped on the rooster during the flight, but all three "passengers" returned to earth unharmed.*

Top right and bottom: *In the nineteenth century, daring spirits took their balloons further and higher. The balloonists featured in the upper picture reached an impressive height of 14,000 feet (4,000 meters).*

A few months later, in November, de Rozier and the Marquis had wafted over Paris in their balloon called "Montgolfiere," making them the world's first aviators.

Heavier than Air

Ballooning quickly caught on, both for sport and warfare. But, even as they moved through the air, the pioneers knew that they were still at the air current's mercy. In a lighter-than-air machine—a balloon—one could only go where the wind blew.

Some inventors tried to control their huge craft with inefficient, steam-powered propellers. But other people had started to wonder if controlled flight could be achieved in machines that were heavier than air. All through the 1800s, flying enthusiasts worked on this revolutionary idea.

They built model gliders that, equipped with wings, sailed through the air like birds. They built gliders big enough to carry people. They also produced model aircraft, powered by steam. One experimented with another source of power, the newly developed gasoline engine. And, all the time, they pondered at the baffling principles that underlay the science of mechanical flight.

By the end of 1903, these scientists, engineers, and intrepid bird-men had come within inches of the final prize: powered flight, controlled by a human operator. But it was Wilbur and Orville Wright—two bicycle-makers from the American midwest—who finally achieved this dream.

The House on Hawthorn Street

Wilbur Wright was born on April 16, 1867, on a farm in Indiana. Orville came into the world on August 19, 1871, in a white frame house in Dayton, Ohio. They were the third and fourth sons of a clergyman, Milton Wright, who was soon to become a bishop. After some shuttling between Ohio, Indiana, and Iowa, the bishop settled down with his wife and children in the Dayton house, and made it the family home.

Wilbur and Orville's childhood seemed rather ordinary. They went to school, and sometimes played hooky. They did household chores to earn some money, and spent what they earned on their hobbies. Wilbur's passion was skating. Orville, an

This engraving shows people testing an "electric anti-gravity" device: another design that never worked! The wheel turned by the aviator in this picture generated static electricity that—in theory—lifted the machine into the air.

entrepreneur, went for schemes like collecting and selling scrap metal.

They also made things. With the help of his friends, Orville did a brisk trade in homemade kites. Wilbur, meanwhile, invented a machine for folding newspapers and made a little money folding the pages of a local church magazine. The process involved eight pages an issue, to be folded and trimmed every week. Wilbur found the work terribly boring and decided he had better things to do with his time. So he automated the process, powering his invention with a treadle of the sort then used for sewing machines.

The Chinese Top

Making things seemed to run in the Wright family. The boys' mother, Susan, could fix almost anything, including a sled she made for her sons. Her husband, the bishop, did not share her practical gifts. But he applauded them in his sons—and encouraged others. He delighted in his children's inquiring minds and wanted to help them explore new ideas. Wilbur and Orville, pursuing one hobby after another, were allowed to take any book they wanted from his library.

The bishop actually introduced them to one of the projects himself, sparking their curiosity about the mysteries of flight. In the late 1870s, he came home one day with a present he had bought for them. He tossed the little object into the air and it soared up to the ceiling.

Today, the bishop's present would be called a model helicopter. It was then known as a "Chinese flying top." It was a propeller on a spindle, powered by pulling on a tightly wound string. Children in Europe had been playing with them since the early 1400s. The Wrights' toy was the very latest model, powered by a twisted rubber band.

The boys played with their top until it broke. Then, fired with enthusiasm, they made copy after copy. They called them "bats." Wilbur, getting more ambitious, made them bigger and bigger, until they were so heavy that they didn't fly.

The Four-Year Gap

Years later, Wilbur would say that he and Orville worked, played, and thought together from childhood. Orville, the more outgoing lad, remembered things differently. Early on, he recalled, they found the four years between them an awkward gap to bridge. Projects like the "bats" had brought them together sometimes, but most of the time Wilbur had stayed immersed in his sports and his books.

School interested Wilbur more than it did his brother. Both of them were bright, but Wilbur enjoyed school work enough to volunteer for extra study in Greek and mathematics. Orville, just as gifted but more rebellious, got into trouble so much that one school actually threw him out.

By this time, the kites had long been replaced by an interest in home printing. With a friend, Orville set up a kitchen-table printing firm, building his own press and producing handbills for Dayton shopkeepers. The venture was so successful that he eventually devoted all of his time to printing during the summer months.

It looked as if the intellectual Wilbur would go one way while Orville, the businessman in the making, would go another. But then something happen to change their lives forever.

The Partnership

The brothers came together as a result of Wilbur's special love of skating—both the style and the skill of figure skating, and the speed of ice hockey. But all skating came to an end when, during an ice hockey match, a team-member's stick smacked him full in the face. The accident cost him all the front teeth in his upper jaw. His face healed—but it was then discovered that he had heart trouble as well. Wilbur said goodbye to the skating rink and the gym, and settled as best he could into the life of a semi-invalid.

Susan Wright—once so resourceful and active—was by then also ill. Immobilized by his own heart trouble, Wilbur spent hours with his mother and looked after her.

Susan Wright died in 1889. The house on Hawthorn Street felt empty now, for the two older boys had also left home. Susan's place in the household was taken by the boys' sister Katharine. The youngest of them all, she cooked and cared for the three men in her family.

At one point before their mother died, Wilbur had offered to help Orville design a new printing press. Although the design was strange, it drew compliments from a professional printer who inspected it. "It works all right," the printer said, "but I don't know why it works."

The Wright Cycle Company

By 1890, Orville was earning his living from printing and publishing a local weekly newspaper. Wilbur soon joined him. But, two years later, they discovered an interest that was more absorbing— bicycling. The craze for cycling was then sweeping Europe and North America. Young people, especially, loved the freedom and independence it gave them, and Wilbur and Orville were no exceptions. Enthralled by their new hobby, they decided to go into business selling bicycles.

In 1892, they set up the Wright Cycle Company. First, they just sold cycles. As the business prospered, they started making and replacing them.

"Early in life the boys showed a mechanical turn of mind and, what was even more important, developed that scientific outlook necessary for pioneers in such a field. They were patient, careful, and painstaking, and never took a step without first making sure that it was theoretically justified. This care was to be of the utmost value when they came to construct their machine."

—John Canning, from "100 Great Lives"

15

The Wright bicycle shop in Dayton, Ohio—the setting in which the world's first airplane was brought into existence. The shop and its contents—like the highly polished desk (right) that Wilbur and Orville used—are now on show at the Henry Ford Museum, Dearborn, Michigan.

In 1897, Orville began to contemplate even grander schemes. In Europe, the engineers Karl Benz and Gottfried Daimler were producing carriages powered, not by horses, but by the newly invented gasoline engine. This, Orville thought, might be even more profitable than making bicycles. But Wilbur, content with the success of their business for now, talked him out if it.

It was just as well—a new hobby had started claiming the brothers' energy. In 1896, they'd heard about another German engineer with a new line of transport. His name was Otto Lilienthal, he was trying to fly—and was succeeding.

Aviation Pioneer: Sir George Cayley

People had, of course, been going up in balloons for over a century. But Otto Lilienthal was experimenting with something else. He was testing flight with a machine that was heavier than air.

Here, too, the story went back for years. It started soon after the first balloon flights, when an English baronet, Sir George Cayley, began a series of experiments in an effort to understand flight. His first one focused on the Chinese top—the same toy that later fascinated the Wright boys. In 1796, he built an improved version that could rise as high as 90 feet (27 meters). Then he started asking himself how things flew.

He studied birds in flight. Then, in 1804, he designed a model glider—based on a common paper kite—that would skim for 60 feet (18 meters) or so through the air. Next came a full-sized one that he successfully launched, unmanned, from a hill. Very much later, he would build an improved model and order his terrified coachman to go up in the glider to see how it flew. The coachman survived, but gave his notice the second he returned to the ground.

"A bird is an instrument working in accordance with mathematical law, which instrument it is within the capacity of man to reproduce."

–Leonardo da Vinci

"It is very beautiful to see this noble white bird sail majestically from the top of a hill to any given point of the plane [sic] below it, according to the set of its rudder, merely by its own weight, descending in an angle of about eighteen degrees with the horizon."

–Sir George Cayley, describing his full-sized glider in flight

17

In 1883, a French artist imagined travel in the future. Although his "air-cars" still looked like lighter-than-air machines, they were powered by the gas engine—just as the Wrights' machine would be.

Power, Weight, and Air

In 1809, Cayley published his findings. In an essay called *On aerial navigation*, he defined heavier-than-air flight in a sentence that became famous. The problem, he wrote, came down to this: making a surface "support a given weight by the application of power to the resistance of the air."

To explain what he meant, he used the example of a bird's wings. As a bird flies forward, its wings meet the air at a slight angle. The wind, which moves horizontally, acts on this angled surface to lift the bird up. It supports the bird's weight—and the bird soars high in the sky.

Cayley's interest in advancing the possibilities of heavier-than-air flight later spread to a textile engineer named William Henson. In 1842, Henson summed up the baronet's thinking much more clearly than Cayley himself had. "If," he wrote, "any light and flat, or nearly flat, article be projected or thrown edgeways in a slightly inclined position, the same will rise on the air till the force exerted is expended."

A flight that never took place. This steam-powered flying machine was invented in the 1840s by William Henson. To drum up publicity (and money) for his project, he had pictures printed that showed the aircraft steaming over London. But, when he tried it out, the test model failed to fly.

This failed design for flight attempted to use pedal power to lift a human into the air.

And it would go on rising—as long as the two conditions were met. Its front edge has to go on being higher than the back one, and the power that moved it forward had to be maintained.

Henson reasoned that what muscle-power did for birds, steam could do for humans. And, in the 1840s, he produced a design for a bird-shaped "Aerial Steam Carriage." It was a breakthrough because, unlike the balloon, it had steam-powered wings that would simulate birds' flight.

When it was tested, Henson's design did not work. Discouraged, he gave up his experiments and emigrated to the United States. But his partner, John Stringfellow, carried on with the work and, in 1848, came up with a new experimental model. Measuring ten feet (3 meters) across from wing-tip to wing-tip, and also powered by steam, it was designed to be launched along a tight-stretched cable.

When tested in an old lace factory, Stringfellow's machine shot along the wire, reached the end, and continued upward under its own power until it flew into the canvas placed to catch it. It was the first powered model aircraft to achieve free flight.

Lilienthal's Obsession

In the 1860s, a boy named Otto Lilienthal joined the pursuit of flight. With his brother, he tried making slip-on wings out of wood. The wings were failures, but the boy went on working at the problem. When he grew up, trying to fly became his obsession.

As an adult design engineer, he realized that all the other inventors had something in common. They knew—or thought they knew—a lot about flight. Flying was a practical activity. The way to learn practical activities, he reasoned, is to do them. And the way to solve the puzzle of flight was to get airborne.

This machine was tested in London. When launched from a height, it instantly crashed to the ground, killing its inventor.

The Hump-Back Curve

Like Cayley before him, Lilienthal started studying birds. In 1889, he published his findings, in a work now thought of as the oldest textbook on mechanical flight. One of the most important things he found out concerned the shape of a flying wing—not its lengthwise shape, but the shape of its cross-section. A section through a bird's outstretched wing is not flat, it is "cambered." It rises in a shallow humped curve, steeper on one side than the other. This shape is called an airfoil, and it is on the airfoil that mechanical flight is based.

When an airfoil—an aircraft wing—is in flight, the air through which it's passing flows both above and below it. Because the airfoil's top surface is bigger than its bottom one, the air there has further to flow. This means that it flows faster.

. . . .

"An object offers as much resistance to the air as the air does to the object."

–Leonardo da Vinci

. . . .

Look carefully at the middle picture of the owl. Can you see the slight upward slant its wings and body make toward the direction it's going? If you look at the aircraft, you can see the same thing. Both types of wing are also airfoils, with a sharp convex curve on their upper side. The "flaps" curving down from the back of the aircraft's wings help slow it down for landing; the extra flap jutting out from the wing's front edge help keep it flying at a slower speed.

Bernoulli's Principle, a law of physics, states that when a moving gas or liquid speeds up, the pressure it exerts on surfaces around it lessens. The air moving over the aircraft wing exerts less pressure on it than the air moving underneath it.

The lower pressure creates a suction effect above the wing, called "lift." As a result, the air moving over the airfoil works from above to pull the airfoil up. Lift is a force that increases as an airfoils forward movement gets faster. So, the faster an aircraft flies, the stronger the upward pull on its wings become. Meanwhile, the air underneath the airfoil is pushing it up from below.

Lift and Drag

An aircraft is always countered by gravity, trying to pull it back to the ground. Another force that

counters the aircraft's forward thrust is called "drag." Drag is the friction resulting from the air through which the airfoil moves. Like lift, it increases with the wing's speed. So, while the air works to pull the aircraft up, it works to pull it back at the same time.

This is where the wing's angle to the air, a slight upward slope, becomes important. The best possible angle is the one that gives the airfoil the biggest amount of lift and the least amount of drag. The angle changes all the time, depending on the speed at which the airfoil is moving. If the angle becomes too flat, the lift decreases and the drag grows. If the angle becomes too sharp, things get dangerous because the lift decreases, the drag increases, and the aircraft stops flying.

This early photograph shows Otto Lilienthal in flight, using his "double decker," or biplane, glider. The Wrights would later adopt the biplane design for their own experiments in flight.

Lilienthal Airborne

In 1891, after years of workbench experiments, Otto Lilienthal began to test the effects of lift and drag on himself. To do this he built an experimental aircraft. It consisted of a glider of willow cane covered with cotton sheeting. Under the wings, it was equipped with padded "sleeves" through which Lilienthal thrust his arms.

With his cotton wings spread out, he climbed onto a springboard, jumped off, and found himself gliding through the air. Before long, he could fly hundreds of yards, then more. Then he discarded the springboard and used steep hills for take-offs. In Berlin, he had a 50-foot (15 meter) artificial hill built for him.

His total number of flights reached the hundreds, then the thousands. And, with each one, his experience at handling the air grew. Lift and drag, he discovered, were not the whole story. He had to keep steady in the air as well. He found he could keep his glider balanced if he carefully moved his dangling body around.

By 1896, when his fame reached the United States—and the Wrights—he was planning a major improvement to his glider. He was going to power it with an engine. But, before he could install it, the great Lilienthal made a single mistake in the air. He tried to correct himself, failed, and—from the height of 50 feet (15 meters)—plunged to his death.

Spellbound

Far away in Dayton, the news of Lilienthal's death and his obsession with flying triggered something in the Wright brothers. Suddenly, they were spellbound by the magical idea of flight. They wanted to know more about it. They wanted a chance to try it for themselves.

The brothers started their research at Dayton Public Library, but found little to help them. Doggedly, they kept on hunting and, in 1899, Wilbur finally wrote for help to the famous Smithsonian Institution in Washington.

The Smithsonian sent him back a reading list that covered much of what had been written on mechanical flight. Its starting point was Leonardo da Vinci, and it ended with the very latest books on the subject. One of these sources was by a

"Otto Lilienthal was the first man to practice gliding persistently and scientifically, as a means whereby the airplane might be perfected, and controlled mechanical flight actually achieved. . . . Without his work, and especially without his example, it is doubtful whether the Wrights would have succeeded."

–C.L.M. Brown, from "The Conquest of the Air"

"Sacrifices will have to be made."

–The dying words of Otto Lilienthal; quoted in the "Wright Papers"

French-born engineer and gliding enthusiast, Octave Chanute, and another by an American, Professor Samuel P. Langley. Langley had been working on mechanical flight for years. In 1896, he had even made a steam-powered model aircraft that had flown three-quarters of a mile over Washington's Potomac River.

Now, at last, the Wright brothers had something to go on. It was summer, and the springtime rush of the bicycle business was easing. So, like students before an exam, they pored over their books, cramming themselves with facts. Fired with enthusiasm, Wilbur and Orville began to think things out for themselves.

The Question of Balance

Workers in production at the Wright's Dayton bicycle shop.

Obviously, the question of balance was crucial. An aircraft that kept tipping from side to side in the

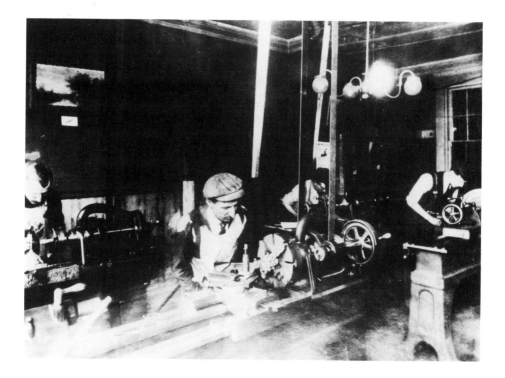

air was worse than useless, it was dangerous. Lilienthal had died because he couldn't balance his flying machine. The Wright brothers wrestled with this problem day and night for months. Soon, they came up with a solution—a completely new one, untried by anyone else.

The answer was to change the shape of the machine's wings during flight.

If, the Wright brothers reasoned, a flying machine tipped over to the left, its left-hand wing would be lower than the right-hand one. If the shapes of the wings could be changed, the left-hand wing could be altered so it met the air at a sharper angle than its right-hand twin. A sharper angle meant greater lift. The left-hand wing would rise, and the right-hand one would sink, and the machine would again be balanced in flight. The idea was on target, but they needed to figure out how to make it work.

A Box for an Inner Tube

At the shop, the peak selling months were almost over, but flat tires were never out of season! One day, a customer came in to buy a new inner tube for his bicycle. Wilbur fetched one, packed in its narrow cardboard box, and took it out. Then, idly turning the box between his fingers, he stood chatting with the purchaser.

Suddenly, he looked at what his hands were doing. They were holding the box at either end, by the corners. And as the chat drifted on, he was twisting the two ends in different directions. One moment, he could see the top left-hand end of the box, and the bottom right-hand one. A twist in the opposite direction, and the top right-hand end came into view.

It dipped down at the back, and started up at the front. . . up at the front.

"By comparison with many more or less contemporary inventions, such as the telephone, the cinematograph, and the transmission and reception of sound waves. . . the flying machine represents, in one sense, the greatest of all; for to solve the problem of mechanical flight it was necessary not so much to observe, as to learn how to defy the immutable law of gravity and actually to fly in the face of Nature."

—M.J.B. Davy

Now, he thought to himself, suppose the box were the right-hand and left-hand wings of an aircraft. How could we make it work?

"Wing-warping"

The day of the inner-tube box marks the true start of the Wright brothers' great pursuit of flight. Like Lilienthal, they knew that the only way to learn about flying was to fly. Luckily, because of the box-wing theory, they could now fly more safely than Lilienthal had.

Wilbur's inspiration decided the pattern their work would follow. During July and August 1899, they built a "double-decker" kite that imitated the box's shape. It measured five feet (1.5 meters) across, and was equipped with cords leading to its corners. Depending on how the cords were pulled, the kite's double wings twisted down at one end or another—just like the box had done.

The sands of Kitty Hawk, North Carolina, were the perfect place for flight trials. Here, Orville (with his back to the camera) and Wilbur are flying their home-made glider as a kite. The small extra "wing" above their heads is the glider's rudder. Attached to the front of the aircraft, it gave the glider fore-and-aft balance.

In August, watched by a group of small boys, Wilbur tried their new kite out on a patch of wasteland outside Dayton. He returned home very satisfied. The idea that the brothers called "wing-warping" worked.

Within a few years, it formed the basis of a patent they would file for their complete system of aircraft control. With the flexible wings replaced by a system of movable flaps, this basic idea is still used by aircraft today.

Enlisting an Expert

Otto Lilienthal, for all his flying knowledge, had only put in approximately five hours of actual practice in the air. Wilbur and Orville planned to have many, many more—and the way ahead was now open. They would build a kite big enough and strong enough to carry a human passenger. In other words, a glider.

But kites need wind. A kite carrying a person needs plenty of wind, strong and steady. A sudden lull would be disastrous! The brothers figured they needed a wind of 15 mph for their experiments. The Wrights first asked Washington's Weather Bureau for information on area wind speed, and received a list of places. Then Wilbur had an even better idea. He wrote to Octave Chanute—and, without knowing it, enlisted their most important ally in their battle against the air.

The Perfect Place

In Chicago, Chanute was delighted to hear from a fellow enthusiast. He wrote back warmly to his correspondent in Dayton, with helpful suggestions. Sand dunes, he said, were an ideal practice ground, partly because sea breezes were reliably steady. How about the coast of California he suggested—or, even better, South Carolina?

"The attitude adopted by the Wright brothers was that every theory previously advanced must be tested and proved by practical experiment, and the courage and thoroughness of their work has been described as a perfect example of the way in which research should be conducted."

—M.J.B. Davy

By this time, it was the spring of 1900. As spring turned into summer, the brothers moved from thinking to action. They began to build their glider. They got out their wind-speed tables again and looked through them. They looked for a place that had coasts, sand dunes, and was not too far from Ohio. One place struck them at once.

Chanute had been almost right. It was on the coast of North Carolina instead of South, on one of the long sandy islands that separated the coastal lagoons from the Atlantic Ocean. It had a weather bureau and two lifeguard stations. Its name was Kitty Hawk, and it was perfect.

Success Above the Sand

By the start of September the brothers had everything ready to go. Orville stayed in Dayton to mind the bicycle shop, while Wilbur set up things on the coast. A few weeks later, it was Orville's turn to leave for North Carolina, taking with him a good supply of groceries. "They can't buy even tea or coffee or sugar at Kitty Hawk," Katharine Wright wrote to their father.

At Kitty Hawk, the wind whipped against the sides of the brothers' tent. Above the flapping came a sizzling noise outside. It was the sand blowing past again, turning the land into more of a desert every day. High above it all, came the dauntless singing of the mockingbird.

On the camp-bed opposite, Wilbur was still asleep. His brother unrolled himself from his blankets, undid the tent flaps, and peered outside.

Orville rubbed his eyes and looked again. Where was the glider? They'd left it only a short distance away. But it was not there now. There was nothing to be seen but sand, mounded up in a smooth, unbroken hump. Exclaiming angrily, Orville came out of the tent at a crouching run.

The Soaring Machine

He found the machine almost at once. On his knees at the edge of the mound, scrabbling frantically, his fingers hit against something hard like a stick. It was only eight inches down, but a heavy layer of sand could do a lot of damage.

Orville dug on furiously. Beside him, a grim-faced Wilbur appeared, and began to dig too.

Slowly, the object they called a "soaring machine" emerged. First came the wooden supports for the elevator, the front rudder they'd built on to give the glider fore-and-aft balance. Working back, they came to the upper wing: 17 feet (5 meters) wide, 5 feet (1.5 meters) deep, humped in a shallow, subtle curve from front to back, and covered with cotton sateen stretched over ashwood ribs. Somewhere down below, past a web of steel wires, was the lower one—also curved and tightly stretched, but with a hole cut out of the middle, facing the rudder.

As the morning wore on, the brothers uncovered the top wing, dug down past the wooden uprights, dusted sand off the pale sateen, and slid the glider free. Anxiously, they checked it over for

This Kitty Hawk photograph shows the launching procedure for gliding. The aviator here is Orville, with Wilbur (left) and a Kitty Hawk man for assistance.

damage. But, miraculously, there was none. The wind—still rushing by at 25 mph—was too good to miss. Lugging their machine between them, the brothers set out on their regular route to the sand dunes.

The Glider Comes Alive

The wind always seemed to be blowing at Kitty Hawk. The week the brothers first tested their glider, it had been blowing off and on at gale force. Sensibly, they dropped their plan to go up in the machine until the wind was calmer.

Instead, they weighted their glider with a chain and flew it on ropes, like a vast kite. They controlled the rudder with cords, pulling this way and that to make the glider dip and rise.

Their creation took on the power and personality of a living thing. Sometimes it behaved beautifully, soaring and dipping to order. Sometimes it went crazy, plummeting earthward. But, by the end of their stay on the sands, Wilbur and Orville felt they truly understood it. They were ready to try flying it.

The brothers now needed an assistant, so they convinced the Kitty Hawk postmaster, Bill Tate. The Tate family had been their friends from the first, feeding them and housing them until they set up camp. The glider's sateen wings had even been finished on Mrs. Tate's sewing-machine.

For the manned gliding session, the Wrights and their helper went to the largest sand dunes on the island. Called Kill Devil Hills, they rose 100 feet (30 meters) above the surrounding flats. It was a perfect launching point for the glider.

For each launch, they'd placed the machine high up on the biggest dune, facing downhill. One of the brothers would climb onto the machine's lower wing, and lie flat in the middle. Tate and the other brother would position themselves at either

···························

"The wind shaking the roof and sides of the tent sounds exactly like thunder. When we crawl out of the tent to fix things outside the sand fairly blinds us. It blows across the ground in clouds. We certainly can't complain of the place. We came down here for wind and sand, and we have got them."

–Orville Wright, in a letter to Katharine Wright, October 1900

···························

32

Despite high winds and an unproven flying machine, Wilbur—here seen in mid-glide—swore that their experiments in the air weren't dangerous.

end of the wings, lift the machine between them, and start running.

As the air started moving over and past the wings, the glider became airborne. The helpers let go, and the machine sailed majestically downhill, to land gently on the sand at the bottom.

Not as Much as a Bruise

In letters, Wilbur assured his pen pal Chanute that their flying experiments were completely safe. Even though the machine sometimes flew at 30 mph, neither he nor Orville got as much as a bruise. Despite their success so far, there were still a lot of things that puzzled them. Lilienthal's figures on lift didn't seem to apply. But, after all, they had only done two minutes of actual manned gliding. They would come back next year and find out more.

In good spirits, Wilbur and Orville set out for home, leaving their machine behind, It was now Bill Tate's, to do with what he liked. Very soon, his two little girls appeared in brand-new dresses of the best French sateen. Mrs. Tate's sewing-machine had been active again.

What's Gone Wrong?

When they went back to Kitty Hawk in July 1901, the brothers were full of confidence. They had built a bigger, more powerful machine. They had the advice and support of Chanute, by now very interested in their project. They even had the company of two of Chanute's proteges, one with medical training.

In their new camp, close to Kill Devil Hills, the Wrights were all set to have a splendid time.

The kitchen in the Wrights' camp building at Kitty Hawk was well stocked by Orville. He taught himself to make scones, using the flour and baking pans shown in the picture.

Instead, they had a worrying one.

Things went wrong from the start. It rained; then the brothers were ill. With the dry weather came clouds of bloodthirsty mosquitoes that plagued the camp day and night. One of Chanute's friends turned out to be a fool and a bore. And—worst of all—the new machine did not fly as well as the old one.

At a moment's notice, the aircraft would go out of control, gusting up and down throughout the dunes. Once, with Wilbur aboard, it rose to 40 feet (12 meters) and almost stopped moving—the same situation that led to Lilienthal's death. Luckily, it recovered from this near-stall, and delivered the startled Wilbur to Earth again.

One problem was with the new camber the brothers had built into the wings. It was the one Lilienthal had used. But it seemed too sharp, too extreme. Wilbur and Orville went back to their original camber—but then had other doubts.

The Wright Cycle Company shop was the birthplace of modern airplane design— with a Dayton undertaker next door.

There were still so many other things they still did not understand.

In August, the Wrights arrived back at home unexpectedly, oddly silent about flying. Wilbur went straight to bed with a cold. Frustrated and depressed, he was about to give up.

Chanute to the Rescue

It was Chanute who came to the rescue. He knew, none better, that the brothers had already broken all gliding records ever made. He'd seen them in action, too, having stayed a week at the Kill Devil camp. They now knew more about flying than anyone else alive—or dead. He was convinced that they had to go on.

Before the month was up, Chanute had cured Wilbur's despair by—very shrewdly—giving him something else to worry about. The elder Wright was invited to give a talk to a grand professional body, the Western Society of Civil Engineers. The subject, of course, was the brothers' flying experiments at Kitty Hawk.

Wilbur came out of his depression instantly. Reserved and modest, he at first wanted to refuse the invitation. But his sister bullied him into accepting. Dressed up in Orville's stylish clothes, Wilbur overcame his stage fright and gave a magnificent lecture.

And he did more. He publicly questioned the value of the figures that had been published so far on mechanical flight.

At home in Dayton, it was Orville's turn to feel nervous. The figures that Wilbur was challenging had been produced by some of the best scientific brains of the time. But the Wrights weren't scientists; they had never gone to college. They'd gotten into flying purely for fun. Orville wondered if they were qualified to make such statements.

Uncharted Territory

There was only one way for Orville to ease his anxiety. He had to re-check those figures for himself. Kitty Hawk was now far away, but that was no problem. He rigged up a miniature wind tunnel in an old box, and spent several hours testing models of curved wing-surfaces. By the end of the day, he had the answer. The published figures were wrong. The question was: by how much?

When Wilbur came back from the presentation, the new riddle proved to be just what he needed to prevent his blues from returning. He and Orville plunged into a large-scale testing project. They built a bigger wind-tunnel and, in an air-current produced by a gas-driven fan, they tested over 200 different sorts of wing surfaces—long ones and short ones; thick ones and thin ones; singles, doubles, even triples, stacked one on top of each other. How did everything behave? Carefully, Wilbur noted the results of their countless experiments and sent their findings off to Chanute—column after column of figures down the pages in neat writing.

The Wrights were entering areas of knowledge where no one—however famous or highly qualified—had ever been before. The brothers only had two months to organize all of their discoveries. By Christmas, it was again time to prepare for the spring bicycle rush. But, by then, they had identified and recorded conditions that would allow a heavier-than-air machine to fly.

Without meaning to, they had joined the foremost ranks of the world's scientific pioneers.

The New Camp

It went without saying that they would go back to Kitty Hawk. By August 1902, they were rushing around the house on Hawthorn Street, sewing wing-covers for a new glider and growing braver

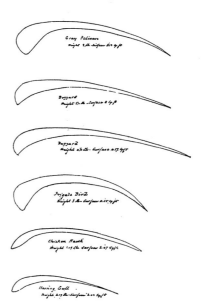

Wing Sections of Stuffed Birds

The key to flight: what a bird's wing looks like when seen from the side. It is also the way air behaves when flowing over a shape like this. The specimens shown here were drawn by the Wrights' friend and expert advisor, Octave Chanute. The curve that the brothers built into the wings of their aircraft was halfway between the buzzard shape (second from top) and the herring bull one (bottom).

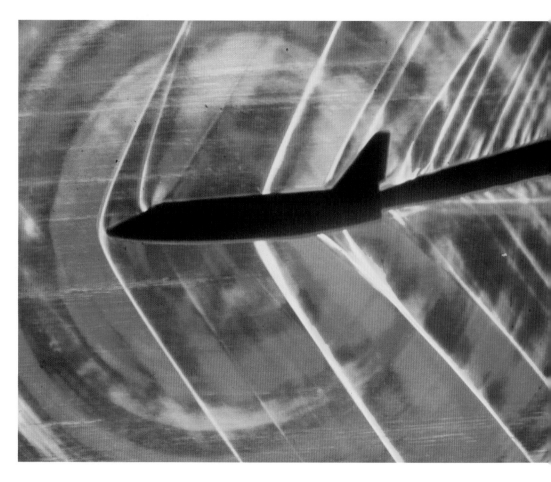

The bottom photograph opposite shows the Wrights' own testing station: the workroom behind the cycle shop, where the homemade wind tunnel stood. The inside of a wind tunnel of the 1970s is shown opposite above, during tests on a space shuttle design. The picture above shows a different test method, a computer simulation of air flow and resistance.

by the day. "They will be all right when they get down in the sand," commented Katharine wisely.

There was another delay when, at the end of the month, they got back to their old camp by the Kill Devil Hills. The sand and winds of Kitty Hawk had half-buried the shed in which they kept their machine, and they had to repair it. They also added a living space for themselves. In September, their flying season could finally start in earnest.

They went up over 1,000 times in their new flying machine. They took off into gale-force winds. They stayed airborne for 40 seconds at a time; then 50 seconds, then a minute. This latest glider, based on their own research, had the lift of a bird and—almost all the time—the control of a well-made glider.

All it needed was power.

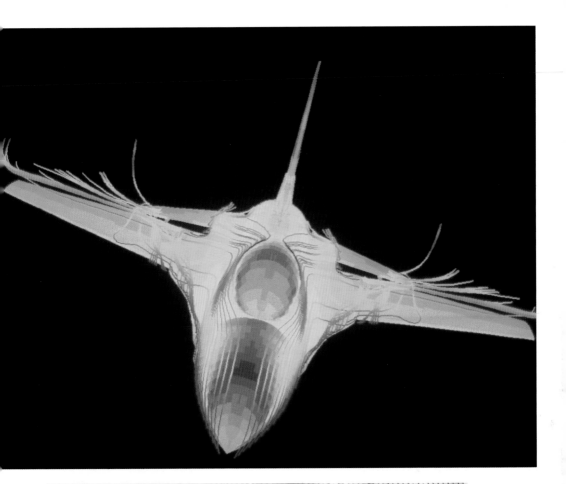

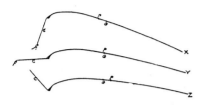

Wilbur used these diagrams in his Chicago lecture to show what happened when an airfoil—the top wing of their glider—was flown as a kite in different strengths of wind. A light wind made it fly up at the end of its cord (top drawing); a very strong one pulled it down.

Power for the Machine

The next step was to get a gas engine, and the brothers turned to the automobile companies for assistance. They wrote letter after letter, asking firms if they would build a very special "one-off"— a very powerful engine that weighed no more than 200 lb. (41 kilograms). Everywhere, they met with disappointment.

So they built one themselves. Amazingly, they got in ready for testing in six weeks. And, when they ran it, they found they'd built a motor that was even lighter and stronger than the one they'd originally asked for.

The propeller gave them more trouble. They planned to copy the design used for ships' propellers but, after more research in Dayton Public Library, the brothers realized they would have to think of another solution. The facts and figures they needed were simply not available. The ship builders of the time didn't design their propellers in advance. They just proceeded by trial and error, stopping when they had a propeller that worked. That was not an option for the Wrights.

Another long research period now faced the brothers. And this time, even they felt daunted by the nightmarish problems involved. A propeller, they reasoned, behaved like an airfoil moving in a spiral course. But how could that movement be observed and tested? As Orville commented later: "It's hard to find even a point from which to make a start; for nothing about a propeller or the medium in which it acts, stands still for a moment."

"The thrust," he went on, "depends on the speed and the angle at which the propeller is turning, the speed the machine is traveling forward, and the speed at which the air is slipping backward; the slip of the air backward depends upon the thrust exerted by the propeller, and the amount of the air acted upon. When any one of these changes, it changes all the rest."

In the end, incredibly, the brothers managed to solve this temporary setback as well. And, when they returned to their practice ground in September 1903, they were again full of confidence and ready to fly.

The First Launch

There were, of course, the usual delays. As before, they found that the Kill Devil camp was the worse for wear. So they did repairs to the old shed, and built a second one beside it. Then, the weather turned stormy, producing winds that—at 75 mph—bordered on hurricane strength. Then it rained; later it snowed.

There were problems with the machine, too. When the motor was tested on the ground, things broke or came loose. Usually, the broken parts had to go back to a shop in Dayton for replacement, but the brothers carried out one on-the-spot repair themselves. They secured the loose parts together with the same rubber cement they used in making bicycle wheels.

At last, by December 14, everything was ready—the aircraft, the launching equipment, and the launch assistants. These were the men of the nearby Kill Devil Lifeguard station, who were fascinated with the experiments the brothers were conducting further up their lonely beach. In the calm of a fine winter's afternoon, they helped the Wrights haul the machine up Big Kill Devil Hill, and adjust its launching rail.

Wilbur and Orville tossed a coin to decide who would try out the machine first, and Wilbur won. He slid into the pilot's place, while Orville steadied it at one end. The engine throbbed; the wires holding the machine in place were released.

"Those who formerly had lifted themselves from the surface of the earth had been too dependent upon the natural forces that they had utilized. . . . The Wrights showed how it was possible to fly into the wind."

—Michael Harrison, from "Airborne at Kitty Hawk"

Before the Wright brothers finally solved the problems of human aviation, only birds knew the true secrets of flight.

The machine, rushing forward, tore itself from Orville's grasp in an instant. An instant more, and it was lifting itself off the rail. It was climbing too far, and losing all of its speed! It stalled.

Sagging back to the ground again, it caught a wing, spun around, and crunched to a halt. The trial was over.

Wilbur had been airborne for just three and a half seconds.

The Machine Flies

The plane was not badly damaged. The front rudder and one of the skids would need some repairs, but that was all. The Wrights now knew that their launching system worked. All in all, things were going well.

They spent the next day and a half doing repairs. By afternoon on December 16, the machine was ready again. During the night, it got colder. When the brothers woke up on Thursday, December 17, the puddles around the camp were covered with ice. And that wasn't the only change. The Kitty Hawk wind had increased and was now blowing from the north at 27 mph (43 kilometers). The brothers got tired of waiting and took their aircraft out on the sand flats by camp to make it fly.

The "Moth out of Season"

With eyes narrowed against the wind, Orville watched as the little aircraft droned on its fourth flight of the day. So did the other witnesses, whose names would later be famous: lifeguards Daniels, W.S. Dough and A.D. Etheridge from Kill Devil; the elderly W.C. Brinkley, who retired to the area; and Johnny Moore, a local youth.

Flying over the sandy beach, the machine looked like some great pale moth—a moth out of season. With its fragile wings, its twirling propellers, and its thrumming engine, it belonged to a world that had not yet come. But, with every turn of the propellers, that world ventured closer and closer to reality.

The plane suddenly darted toward the ground. After a bumpy take-off, Wilbur had been doing so well. But now the machine was pitching up and down, just as it had done on its first flight. It made one final swoop, hit the ground, and stayed motionless.

No doubt about it, this was the longest flight yet. Something like 800 feet (244 meters); more maybe. In their glider a year ago, they'd been happy to travel half that distance.

On December 17, 1903 at 10:35 in the morning, Orville took off to make the world's first flight in a power-driven, heavier-than-air machine. Wilbur, who steadied the plane while it moved down the launching rail from the left, is still half running in this photo: the prop that held the wing up is in the middle of the picture.

Joyously, Orville and the rest of the group hurried over to the sands where Wilbur and the machine waited for them. The plane showed signs of a rough landing. The front rudder was smashed, but it could be easily repaired. The brothers and their helpers carried the machine back to camp in good spirits, and stood around for awhile, talking about the impressive results of the day.

"Inform Press Home Christmas"

Suddenly, as they talked, disaster struck. An extraordinary gust of wind came tearing along the sand, caught the aircraft, and flipped it over. Grabbing where they could, everyone dived to the rescue. But the machine rolled over and over, taking lifeguard John Daniels with it. When finally helped to his feet, he was bruised and shaken. But the aircraft had come off much worse. The wings were buckled, their wooden ribs smashed, the engine damaged. There would be no more flying for the Wright brothers that year.

But there would always be next year. And all the years to come. The brothers were not discouraged. Four powered flights were enough for now.

Vanishing into their shed, Wilbur and Orville Wright made lunch, ate it, washed the dishes, and set off to Kitty Hawk to send a telegram back to Dayton. "Success four flights Thursday morning," it read. "Inform press home Christmas."

The Story that Went Begging

In Dayton, the Wright family did as the brothers asked. They informed the press, who were not particularly interested. Meanwhile on the coast, an enterprising young journalist heard of the Wrights' achievement from a telegraph operator. He, too, tried to sell the story to the newspaper but, for the most part, they weren't interested either. Only three papers printed the story the next morning—and they did not include Dayton's own *Journal*!

The story of the year had passed them by, and few people realized it. Astonishingly, it would be five years before the fame the brothers deserved caught up with them.

Between 1903-1908, the Wrights went on with their great flying project in full view of anyone who cared to take notice.

Two forces were at work in keeping this communication gap so big. For a start, the journalists, government officials, and millions of ordinary people who had not seen the Wrights fly simply did not believe that they had.

The world, they all agreed, was full of cranks, claiming they could fly like angels—and so far, these claims had always been false. Powered flight was one of the ultimate challenges facing scientists, and everyone knew progress was slow. Why, that very year, even Professor Samuel Langley had twice failed to make his new machine fly.

....

"With all the knowledge and skill acquired in thousands of flights in the last ten years, I would hardly think today of making my first flight on a strange machine in a twenty-seven-mile wind, even if I knew that the machine had already been flown and was safe. After these years of experience I look with amazement upon our audacity in attempting flights with a new and untried machine under such circumstances."

–Orville Wright, describing the first powered flight at Kitty Hawk on December 17, 1903

....

A World of Non-believers

The people who had seen the Wrights fly were in a different position. They knew they could believe the evidence before their eyes. What they did not understand was the importance of that evidence.

Many of the Wright brothers' witnesses were ordinary working people. Most of them had little to do with the wider world of the news media, let alone that of aviation. They vaguely knew that people were trying to fly. They'd also heard that a rich Brazilian named Alberto Santos-Dumont was flying around the Eiffel Tower.

Of course, they also knew the Wright brothers were flying around the sands of Kitty Hawk as well. But they did not realize that there was a major difference between the exotic Brazilian's machine and that of their own home-grown aviators. Santos-Dumont was flying the very latest lighter-than-air machine: a balloon with an engine attached. The Wrights' aircraft was the very first successful, full-scale, powered, heavier-than-air craft; the world's first airplane.

"The Boys Are At It Again"

In one way, this lack of publicity was a blessing in disguise for Wilbur and Orville. It meant that they could get on with their flying without interruptions. In 1904, they built a new, stronger aircraft—*Flyer II*, as they called it—to replace the mangled but triumphant *Flyer I* of Kitty Hawk. Then they set up a new practice ground: a cow pasture eight miles outside of Dayton, called Huffman Prairie. Here, during the next two years, they brought the art of flying to an astonishing level of expertise.

Two roads and a railway ran past the prairie, so the brothers were never short of passers-by who wanted to witness their acrobatics. The flights

were getting longer so, to stay within the limits of the field, the Wrights taught themselves to turn in the air. They started to circle the field.

By late summer 1905, the brothers' flight mileage entered double figures. In September, the grandson of *Flyer I—Flyer III*—achieved an uninterrupted flight of 12 miles (19 kilometers). Within a few days, this record looked puny beside the new one *Flyer III* had set—24 miles (38.5 kilometers), flown in 38 minutes.

The local onlookers took the Wright brothers' achievements calmly. Calmest of all was their next-door neighbor, a farmer named Amos Stauffer. For Stauffer, the Wrights were just part of the land-scape. "Well, the boys are at it again," he'd say when he saw the *Flyer* in action. Interviewed by a visitor in 1905, he recalled that he "just kept stooking corn until I got down to the fence, and the durned thing was still going round. I thought it would never stop."

The early work of the Wright brothers was often dismissed as madness—but is was the beginning of a new era. This passenger-carrying aircraft is a common sight today but was only a fantastic dream in 1903.

Is the Army Interested?

In another way, the ignorance that cloaked the Wrights' accomplishments was not a blessing, but a curse. The brothers had to earn a living. Wilbur and Orville now knew that they had invented something of value: something that might be very useful to business or to the government.

Naturally, they wanted to give their own government the first option to use their invention. They told their member of congress that they had invented a machine that could be used in war, for "scouting and carrying messages." Would the army be interested in such a vehicle?

For a long while, the U.S. Army reacted just as the United States' press did. They didn't believe a word of it. In Europe, however, the government was less short-sighted. The British started making inquiries about what the Wrights had to sell. So did the French.

In France and Germany, questions had also begun to be asked in aviation circles. Slowly, the publicity that Americans had denied the Dayton brothers was building abroad.

Wheelings and Dealings

The French aviators got so interested that they sent someone on a fact-finding mission to Dayton to see the Wrights in person. This was the visitor who, in 1905, talked to farmer Stauffer. "Claims completely verified," was the message he sent back to France at the end of his trip.

Soon, the Wrights were deep in negotiations with the French, and in 1906, the European connection became even more active. That year and the next, the brothers visited France, then Germany. The air-minded Germans were already developing their great *Zeppelin* airships; now they were interested in aircraft as well!

Wilbur was famous for the total attention he paid to any technical problem, however small. Here, he concentrates on a kite belonging to the son of pilot Frank Coffyn (left).

Meanwhile, the United States Army was at last beginning to come around. Just before Christmas in 1907, in an invitation clearly aimed at the Wrights, it asked anyone who could supply flying machines to state their terms.

In the early months of 1908, deals were now close with both the United States government and a group of top-level French businessmen. But, before anything was settled, both wanted to see the new invention in action. So, in May, Wilbur set off for France, while Orville remained at home to do the official United States trials at Fort Myer.

Wilbur's French visit turned into triumphal progress through Europe, which lasted into 1909. When Orville later joined him, it would be a very different set of adventures.

Wilbur Conquers France

Wilbur's tour started in Le Mans where, on August 8, he began trial flights on a local race course. The crowds who turned out to greet him went wild with enthusiasm. The thin American really could do what he promised—he had indeed conquered the air! And, within a few days, he had conquered the French, too. Unassuming, patient, and good-natured, he won over everyone who met him.

The workers in the factory where he assembled his aircraft were deeply touched by his democratic style. He worked the same hours as them, and ate at the same place. Meanwhile, businessmen, journalists, and aviators vied with each other in their admiration. Women were completely bowled over by the dashing aviator with the lean face and the broad smile. Fan mail poured in by the sackful.

Wilbur bore all of the publicity and attention very well. In September, he even relaxed enough to admit that Madame Berg, wife of one of his French hosts, "was a jolly woman and very intelligent."

Orville (left) watches a flight at Le Mans with English balloonist Griffith Brewer. While visiting with the Wrights in France, Brewer became the first Englishman ever to fly in an airplane.

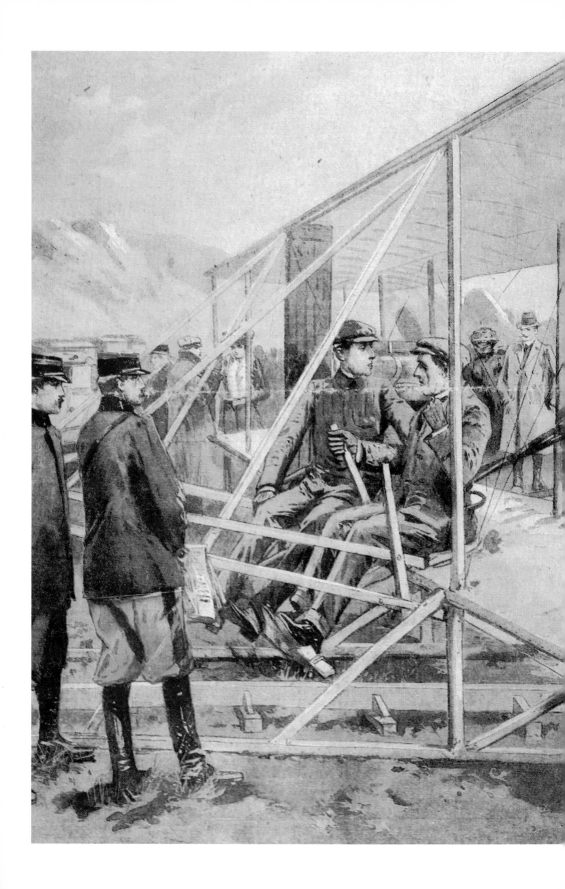

She would later become the first woman ever to go up in an airplane. But then, only a few days later, news would reach him from the United States that ended his cheerfulness.

First Blood

Back in the States, Orville's summer had been going well, too. When, in August, he arrived in Fort Myer for the trials, he was dismayed to find that the flying area was very small. However, he turned the problem into an advantage, and astounded the crowds with the performances he extracted with his aircraft.

The records set on Huffman Prairie dwindled into nothingness; Orville was quickly notching up flights over an hour and rising to heights of over 200 feet (61 meters) and more. The army deal looked like more and more of a certainty.

Then, on September 17, 1908, the unthinkable happened.

Orville's Disaster

Orville had already taken two passengers aloft. Now a third wanted to go: Lieutenant Thomas Selfridge, aged 26. For the first few minutes of the flight, all went well. Then Orville began to sense something was wrong with the machine. He was about to start a hurried descent when, abruptly, it veered out of control.

Desperately, Orville fought to bring the machine down safely. But gravity, in the end, was stronger.

The plane crashed head long into the ground. Selfridge, whose skull was fractured, died later that day in the hospital. By some miracle, Orville escaped with no more than a broken leg, broken ribs, and an injury that went undiagnosed for 12 years—three hip fractures. The crash was the first fatal accident in aviation history.

Opposite: Although protocol kept the King of Spain firmly grounded during his visit, Wilbur was still able to teach him how the Flyer's controls worked. By this time, the Wrights and their passengers flew sitting up. But, once they were airborne, there was still very little to keep them in the plane.

Below: *The accident at Fort Myer, reconstructed by a French artist. The caption reads: "The bird-men: the aviators' terrible crash."*

Le Petit Parisien
Supplément Littéraire Illustré

LES HOMMES-VOLANTS
TERRIBLE CHUTE D'AVIATEURS

Because of Selfridge's death, Wilbur cancelled trials for a few days. He felt personally responsible for the tragedy. If he'd been at Fort Myer, he could have taken some of the weight off Orville's shoulders; helped with the preparation, the checking, or the time-consuming chats with visitors. But the inner toughness that, long ago, had pulled him out of the illness and depression again came to his rescue. He accepted the guilt—and got on with the job.

Glory Days

In his hospital bed in the United States, Orville was being just as tough-minded. Someone asked if he'd lost his nerve. Far from it he replied—the only thing that worried him was getting well in time to finish the army tests the following year.

In November, he came out of the hospital. In early 1909, he joined Wilbur in France, taking with him the staunch Katharine. Because of winter, flying operations had been moved to Pau, in southwestern France.

By now, a French company had been set up to deal in Wright planes. Wilbur's main job was training its pilots. Although Orville and Katharine were put up in Pau's best hotel, he went on sleeping in the hangar beside his plane, just as he had at Le Mans. Quickly, it became the most-visited shed in France—and visitors got grander by the day.

King Alfonso of Spain and King Edward VII of Britain came to see his flying machine. So did Lord Northcliffe, owner of the British newspaper, the *Daily Mail,* who later that year would stage a competition for pilots to fly the English Channel. The race was won by the French aviator Louis Bleriot, in his own monoplane *Bleriot XI.* By now, encouraged by what they'd heard of the Wrights' work in the United States, the French were also developing an aircraft of their own.

King Alfonso longed to go up in Wilbur's impressive flying machine. But he was prevented by his wife and his government ministers. However, no such restrictions weighed on Katharine Wright, who went up twice.

From Pau, the Wrights went on to Italy, where they flew before King Emmanuel. Here, deals to sell the Wright plane got underway, and Wilbur started training Italian fliers. While he was at it, he was approached again by the Germans, whose interest had been growing steadily. Now they wanted to set up a Wright plane company, too. The Wrights had become an international success.

Dayton Welcomes Its Own

Crowned heads of nations, business deals, medals, presentations: these now became everyday features of the Wrights' lives. In May 1909, they went back to the States, where their home town was waiting for them. The people of Dayton, making up for their earlier lack if excitement, staged an official "welcome" that lasted two days.

The brothers and Katharine left the station in a lantern-lit carriage procession, and 10,000 people crowded to meet them at Hawthorn Street. But this was nothing compared to the celebrations the following month. On June 17, all the bells and factory whistles in Dayton sounded at once. Flags flew, bands played, and Wilbur and Orville rode in procession through the wildly cheering crowds. In the evening, there were fireworks. The next day there were two more parades, and the brothers received medals from Congress, from the state of Ohio, and from their own home city.

What Happened to the Joy?

For the Wrights, Dayton's celebration was only one fixture among many on a hectic schedule. The

Wilbur, here seen piloting his sister Katharine, gets ready to fly in his usual flat cap and leather jacket. Katharine has tied a string around her skirts to stop them from flapping. Visible in the background are one of the Flyer's propellers and the uprights of its back rudder, or tail.

Top and opposite:
The first World War of 1914–1918 speeded up aircraft development dramatically. In both pictures, the airplanes look much more like a modern aircraft than the Wrights' machines did. The third picture (opposite bottom) shows war aircraft being used over Mexico.

cheers had hardly died down before the Wrights were back in Washington, completing their trials at Fort Myer. No sooner had the army deal been triumphantly completed when Orville and Katharine set off to Europe again. They were bound for Berlin, where Orville would start a training course for German fliers of the Wright machine. Here he met the famous Count von Zeppelin and the German royal family. Meanwhile, in New York, Wilbur raised American air-mindedness another notch by flying an impressive 21 miles (34 kilometers) along the Hudson River.

Orville and Katharine returned at the start of November; by the end of it, the United States had its own Wright Company, and this made the brothers' schedule even more crowded. There were pilots to train, a factory to build and run (in Dayton of course), aircraft to test, and flying exhibitions to give, stirring up public interest further.

It was very hard work. And, sadly, the Wrights found that they were being taken further and further from what they wanted to do. As they had learned in the exhilarating days of Kitty Hawk, flying was their joy; research their delight. And

Orville in later life, here dressed in the classic aviator's garb of leathers and close-fitting helmet.

now they had become wealthy businessmen, striking deals and fighting designers who infringed on their patents. For company president Wilbur, who dealt with the legal worries, chances to fly were scarce.

In May 1910, Wilbur went up by himself for a short spin over Huffman Prairie, in what would be his last flight. Twenty-four months later, on May 30, 1912, he died from typhoid fever. He was just 45 years old.

Orville Alone

For Orville, the surviving partner, life carried on. He took Wilbur's place as president of the company, and tended to its business. In 1915, he sold all of his interest in it. Then he went back to the research that he and Wilbur had loved so much. He met people like the car manufacturer Henry Ford and the pilot Charles Lindbergh, who in 1927, was the first person to fly solo from New York to Paris.

His family ties that had sustained the great partnership were still intact. He still had his two other brothers and their children; he still had his devoted sister Katharine, and his father.

Indeed Bishop Wright had now become a flier like the rest of them. Orville took their father up for his very first experience in the air in 1912. They reached 350 feet (107 meters).

Two years after Wilbur's death, Orville moved with his father and sister into a large new house outside of Dayton, called Hawthorn Hill. Setting it up had been the last project that he and Wilbur had worked on together. Bishop Wright died in 1917, and Katharine married and moved away in the 1920s. But Orville stayed there for the rest of his life, watching as the gift he and Wilbur had given humanity changed the world beyond recognition.

The Legacy

Even before Wilbur's death, flying had begun to change the world. In 1909, Bleriot flew the English Channel in his monoplane, easily passing the steamship sent to escort him. In 1910, a British pilot hit on the novel idea of carrying letters by air.

The same year, an Ohio department store hired a Wright plane to make the world's first-ever express delivery by air: a roll of silk, carried at the speed of over a mile a minute. Only the very fastest cars could do better—but they had to go where the roads took them. And an express train, like the *Twentieth Century Limited,* running between New York and Chicago, was slower. It took about 20 hours to cover its 1,000 miles of iron tracks.

Already, ideas of time and distance were beginning to change. It felt as if the world was starting to shrink.

Unlike the Americans, the governments of Europe had been quick to spot the military potential of the flying machines. When World War I broke out in 1914, aircraft were already being built that could fly 90 mph (144 kph). By the end of the war, Europe's airspace was ruled by fighter planes like the German *Fokkers* and the British *Sopwith Camel,* with its top speed of 113 mph (182 kph). Meanwhile, the heavier machines used for bombing had begun to fly hundreds of miles at a time.

It was a converted bomber that, in 1919, the British-based aviators John Alcock and Arthur Whitten Brown made the world's first flight across the Atlantic—a distance of almost 1,900 miles (3,058 kilometers). It took them three minutes short of 16 hours. Less than 100 years earlier, when people crossed the Atlantic in sailing ships, it had taken 23 days. It still took four days in the fastest luxury liners of the 1930s.

Pneumatici Dunlop

SOCIETA ITALIANA **DUNLOP**
MILANO ROMA
Via G. Sartori, 32 Via Castro Pretorio 10?

A high-fashion occasion for rich Italians: an air show held in 1928. By now, wealthy people like the ones shown here could experience flying for themselves, in aircraft built for passenger travel.

. . . .

"They had not only made the first wind-tunnel in which miniature wings were accurately tested, but were the first men in all the world to compile tables of figures from which one might design an airplane that could fly. Even today. . . the refinements obtained over the Wrights' figures for the same shapes of surfaces are surprisingly small."

–Fred C. Kelly, from his biography, "The Wright Brothers"

. . . .

Above: *With the narrow "delta" shape of its backswept wings outlined by scaffolding, the supersonic airliner Concorde undergoes maintenance. The space shuttle, shown right, has the same sweptback outline.*

After the war, people realized that long-range aircraft could make money as a mode of travel.

The old bombers were quickly converted to passenger aircraft and, in the 1920s and 1930s, a whole new transport system was offered to those who could afford it. Organized air travel had added itself to the far older (and slower) options of travel by land and sea.

World War II, when it started in 1939, again gave extra impetus to the development of flight. One by one, inventions that had been born in

Dusseldorf Airport, Germany: tended by airport staff, the huge passenger jets of today gleam sleekly in the sun. The scene seems a whole world away from Kitty Hawk and the Kill Devil Hills.

peacetime received their first full use in war: radar, the jet engine, the helicopter.

Orville Is Gone

Orville Wright died, aged 76, on January 30, 1948, three years after aircraft had been used to drop the deadliest weapon of war ever invented: the atomic bomb.

He had already lived to see politicians hurrying around the world in his invention, making decisions that would affect millions. He had seen it used for advertising, trailing messages to boost a business's sales. In Europe, it carried the wealthy from one tourist spot to another; in Australia, it brought medical aid to isolated sheep stations.

Thanks to the Wrights' legacy, we now live in a world where we can eat strawberries in the winter. If we jet off to Chile, we can also go skiing in June. If illness threatens the life of someone in France, a rare drug can be flown in from Japan to help. If there is a wedding on one side of the world, a mother can be there. When disaster strikes a country anywhere on earth, planes can bring in food, medicines, and rescue workers.

When Wilbur and Orville Wright launched their *Flyer I* at Kitty Hawk in 1903, the peoples of the world were kept apart as much by distance and time as by their warring beliefs. Today, both distance and time have lost their power to divide—and rule.

"Achievement followed achievement in the air with such bewildering rapidity that, by the year 1948 when Orville Wright died, the world could no longer marvel. But then, what flight that ever followed—no, not even man's rocketing into space—could match the wonderful achievement and sheer courage of those first breathless twelve seconds in the air that memorable day in December 1903, or equal it in significance as the herald of a new age?"

—John Canning, from "100 Great Lives"

Glossary

Airfoil (also aerofoil)
The shape in which an
aircraft wing is built.
When seen in cross-
section, this shape is
curved above and flat
below. At the front of the
wing, the curve dips
sharply down to a
rounded edge.

Bernoulli's Principle
A physical law stating that
if a moving fluid or gas
moves faster, the pressure
it exerts decreases. It is the
basic law underpinning the
science of aerodynamics,
or the way moving gases
and objects behave when
they interact.

Camber The hump-
backed curve made by the
top of an airfoil; the curve
can be of many different
shapes, from steep to
shallow.

Chinese Flying Top
A spinning top equipped
with an airscrew or
propeller; when spun
quickly, the propeller
carries the top into the air,
just as the rotors do on a
modern helicopter.

Drag Friction between
the air and a moving
aircraft wing, acting to
hold the aircraft back.
One of the four forces
always in action on a
moving, heavier-than-air
machine.

Elevator A movable part
of an aircraft that controls
upward and downward
movement.

Flaps Moveable sections
of a modern airplane
wing, giving control over
lift and drag.

Free flight Occurs
when a heavier-than-air
machine can be kept by
its own power on a level
or upward course, and
continue further on this
course than the distance
that it could glide
unpowered.

Gale force Among
the most violent gusts
on the Beaufort scale
used for measuring wind.
(They range from 32-63
mph).

Glider A heavier-than-air
flying machine without a
built-in power supply.
After taking off, the
machine slowly flies
forward and downward,
pulled by gravity.

Heavier-than-air flight
Flight in aircraft, such as
airplanes, gliders, or
helicopters.

Lift The force that
"sucks" an aircraft wing
upward, originating in the
unequal pressures exerted
by the air moving over
and under the wing.

Lighter-than-air flight
Flight in hot-air balloons
or balloons filled with
some other gas, such as
helium.

Montgolfière A hot-air
balloon, as developed by
the Montgolfier brothers
of France in the
eighteenth century.

Propeller A circular
arrangement of airfoils,
fixed onto a center rod. As
the rod is turned, the
propeller blades are
sucked forward.

Skids The runners of the
sled-like undercarriage of
the Wrights' *Flyer.*

Smithsonian Institution
A famous body that was
set up in Washington in
1864 to promote learning.

Stall For an aircraft to fly,
it has to be moving fast
enough through the air. If
it slows down too much,
it will stall and stop flying.

Wing-warping The system
invented by the Wright
brothers to control the lift
of their aircraft wings, by
changing the shape each
presented to the air.

Zeppelin A huge, sausage-
shaped, lighter-than-air
flying machine, or airship,
developed at the start of
the twentieth century.

Important Dates

1783	**Nov 21:** The first manned flight is staged in a hot-air balloon, developed by the Montgolfier brothers of Annonay, France.
1804	The British inventor, Sir George Cayley, builds first glider—the world's first practical heavier-than-air flying machine.
1842	In Britain, William Samuel Henson patents a design for an airplane, his "Aerial Steam Carriage."
1848	In Britain, John Stringfellow's model airplane is successfully flown, indoors and out.
1867	**April 16:** Wilbur Wright is born near Millville, Indiana.
1871	**August 19:** Orville Wright is born in Dayton, Ohio.
1892	Wilbur And Orville set up their Wright Cycle Company in Dayton, Ohio.
1896	The German aviation pioneer, Otto Lilienthal, dies in a glider crash.
1899	**July-August:** The Wrights make successful experiments with "wing-warping" and a kite.
1900	The Wrights' first glider trials are held at Kitty Hawk, North Carolina.
1901	**July-August:** The Wrights' second glider trials are held at the Kill Devil Hills, four miles south of Kitty Hawk. The Wrights are puzzled and discouraged by the mixed results achieved. **September:** In Chicago, Wilbur addresses the Western Society of Civil Engineers. In Dayton, Orville starts wind tunnel experiments.
1902	Successful trials of the glider based on the Wrights' wind-tunnel research are held at the Kill Devil Hills.
1903	**September-November:** At the Kill Devil Hills, the Wrights assemble their new, power-driven flying machine in readiness for their fourth set of flying trials. **October 17:** Professor S.P. Langley tries out his full-sized, steam-powered airplane (called the aerodrome) over the Potomac River; it fails to fly. A second trial in December also ends in failure. **December 17:** At the Kill Devil Hills, Wilbur and Orville Wright make the world's first powered, manned, self-launching, controlled and successfully sustained flights in heavier-than-air machines.
1904-5	With improved machines, the Wrights continue their flying trials at Huffman Prairie, Dayton, Ohio.
1905-7	Interest in the Wrights' achievement grows, both in Europe and the United States.
1908	August: Wilbur starts highly successful flying demonstrations in France. **September 17:** Orville is injured in flying trials staged for U.S. Army. His passenger, Thomas Selfridge, is killed: the first fatality in airplane flying.
1909	**July:** French aviator Louis Bleriot flies the English Channel, taking 43 minutes to cover 31 miles (50 kilometers). **November:** In the United

States, the Wright Company is set up to build airplanes, and is instantly successful.

1912   **May 30:** Wilbur Wright dies, aged 45, after a sudden illness.

1914-18 World War I gives dramatic impetus to aircraft design and production.

1919   In an adapted Vickers-Vimy bomber, John Alcock and Arthur Whitten Brown become the first people to fly across the Atlantic. The flight of 1,890 miles (3,041 kilometers) takes 15 hours, 57 minutes.

1939   World War II breaks out. Once again, aircraft development is speeded up.

1945   World War II ends when atomic bombs are dropped in Hiroshima and Nagasaki in Japan.

1948   **January 30:** Orville Wright dies, aged 76.

For More Information

Books

Berliner, Don. *Before the Wright Brothers* (Space & Aviation). Minneapolis, MN: Lerner Publications Co., 1990.

Graham, Ian. *Aircraft* (Built for Speed). Chatham, NJ: Raintree/Steck-Vaughn, 1998.

Jefferies, David. *Fliers and Flying Machines* (Timelines). Danbury, CT: Franklin Watts, Inc., 1991.

Lomask, Milton; Pope John Paul II. *Invention and Technology* (Great Lives). Old Tappan, NJ: Antheum, 1992.

Turvey, Peter; David Salariya. *Inventions: Inventors & Ingenious Ideas* (Timelines). Danbury, CT: Franklin Watts, Inc., 1992.

Videos

A & E Home Video. *First to Fly.*

A & E Home Video. *Wilbur and Orville Wright.*

Web Sites

Inventors Gallery—See many early inventors and their contributions to the pursuit of flight: hawii.cogsci.vivc.edu/invent/inventor_gallery.html

Smithsonian National Air and Space Museum—Browse through 23 main galleries, all exhibiting historic aircraft: www.nasm.si.edu

The Wright House: Orville & Wilbur Wright—Many interesting photographs and links are included in this site dedicated to the brothers who conquered the air: www.wam.umd.edu~stwright/WrBr/Wrights.html

Index